Mamie and Papi's

Basic French Grammar

THE PRESENT TENSE

Jean and John Beaver

Tralco-Lingo Fun

Helping to teach and motivate

www.tralco.com

Published under license in the UK by Brilliant Publications

Author	Jean and John Beaver
Illustrator	Nick Thornborrow
Cover Design	Anthony Hughes Productions
Set up Design	Jeremy Major
Publisher	Karen Traynor

We acknowledge the financial support of the government of Canada through the Book Publishing Industry Development Program (BPDIP), a program of the Department of Canadian Heritage.

Published by Tralco Educational Services Inc., Hamilton ON
Telephone 905 575 5717 • Toll free 1 888 487 2526
Fax: 905 575 1783 • Web site www.tralco.com or www.lingofun.com
Original ISBN 978-1-55409-383-0

Legal deposit National Library, Ottawa, Canada

This version available in the UK and Eire
Printed in the UK
ISBN 978-0-85747-154-3

TABLE OF CONTENTS

About the authors

Born and educated in the UK, Jean Beaver has had wide experience teaching in France, England and Canada at the Primary, Intermediate and Secondary levels. Since her retirement she has been a contributor to Tralco-Lingo Fun as a writer, proof-reader, translator, and preparer of commentaries, questions and activities for videos in both English and French.

John Beaver was born and educated in the UK, and has taught French at the secondary and post-secondary levels. Since his retirement from Hillfield-Strathallan College, Hamilton, where he was Director of Arts, he has published "You Mean I Have to Know This?", a series of notes and exercises in French grammar, and has been a contributor to Tralco-Lingo Fun as editor and proofreader.

- 1 -

REGULAR -ER VERBS (PRESENT)

Question! Why do we call them *-er* verbs?

Good question!

Answer: They end in *-er* in their basic or *infinitive* form.

The *infinitive* of the verb is the "to _______" form,
e.g. to sing, to dance, to play (video games!)

In English, we don't use the infinitive after a subject. If you said "I to sing" to your friends, they would think you're weird, right?

Here's the easy part! They don't do that in French either!

So what rules do these "action words" follow?

First let us ask you a question! What is wrong with the following?

he play   she sing

Of course you know the answer; the verbs need an ENDING. In this case, the ending is 's':

he play**s**   she sing**s**

Guess what? You do the same in French, but with more endings!

So do you just add the endings to the infinitive?

NOOOOOOO!

First you take off the -er part. That leaves you with what we call the **stem** of the verb. (the ending is the flower?)

So: if the infinitive of the verb is *chant***er**; the stem is *chant-*.

Then add the endings (each subject adds its own ending).

Singular	Plural
je chant**e**	nous chant**ons**
tu chant**es**	vous chant**ez**
il chant**e**	ils chant**ent**
elle chant**e**	elles chant**ent**

Now, there's one thing that you must remember; only the **-ons** and **-ez** endings are pronounced! Strange, isn't it? But you must still write the endings, even if they aren't pronounced!

That was easy, right? Congratulations! You have just learned the present tense of about 10,000 French verbs, Yeah!

Here are 20 of them for you to learn and to use immediately!

adorer	to love	**donner**	to give
aimer	to like, to love	**écouter**	to listen to
chanter	to sing	**étudier**	to study
coller	to stick, to glue	**fermer**	to close, to shut
colorier	to colour	**jouer**	to play
copier	to copy	**marcher**	to walk
danser	to dance	**montrer**	to show
découper	to cut out	**parler**	to speak, to talk
dessiner	to draw	**regarder**	to look at, to watch
détester	to hate	**sauter**	to jump

USEFUL NOTE!

An interesting and helpful fact is that lots of English verbs that end with the syllable "-ate" are *-er* verbs in French. Here are a few French verbs; what is the English for them? (Don't forget the "to__________".)

décorer ____________________ démontrer ____________________

contempler ____________________ naviguer ____________________

hésiter ____________________ éliminer ____________________

Here are a few English verbs. Write the French equivalent!

to calculate ____________________ to formulate ____________________

to imitate ____________________ to estimate ____________________

to adulate ____________________ to propagate ____________________

Now, here are some exercises you should do to make absolutely sure that you know all the right endings.

EXERCISE A

Put the right ending on the following verbs; here are some examples:

je copi*e* nous aim*ons* tu chant*es* elles dessin*ent*

Now, here we go!

je chant ____

tu écout____

elles ador____

nous saut____

ils arriv____

nous donn____

vous march____

je décor____

ils montr____

elle ferm____

il détest____

tu ferm____

nous ferm____

ils découp____

je parl____

elle colori____

nous regard____

il coll____

elle saut____

elles aim____

EXERCISE B

Now, write out the whole verb!

(copier) je   je *copie*   (aimer) nous   nous *aimons*

Easy, isn't it? Here we go!

(calculer) vous ____________________   (jouer) ils ____________________

(étudier) il ____________________   (détester) elle ____________________

STOP! Did you put the right endings on the verbs? Go back and check!

All right? Then you may proceed!

(chanter) vous ____________________   (donner) je ____________________

(dessiner) nous ____________________   (marcher) tu ____________________

(écouter) elles ____________________   (coller) il ____________________

(montrer) ils ____________________   (fermer) je ____________________

(découper) nous ____________________   (arriver) nous ____________________

(parler) tu ____________________   (étudier) vous ____________________

(jouer) ils ____________________   (danser) nous ____________________

(sauter) elles ____________________   (regarder) vous ____________________

Mamie and Papi's
Basic French Grammar

EXERCISE C

Papi has put the wrong endings on these verbs. Can you make them right for him? Write the whole verb.

Il aimons	____________	nous chante	____________
elles joue	____________	il étudiez	____________
tu saute	____________	nous danses	____________
nous ferme	____________	je découpons	____________
elles marche	____________	ils donnez	____________
tu arrivez	____________	ils colle	____________
nous dessine	____________	j'aimez	____________
nous copies	____________	vous détestent	____________
il découpez	____________	elle parlons	____________
tu écoutent	____________	je montres	____________

EXERCISE D

OK, now you are ready to use the verbs in proper sentences! We'll give you the infinitive; you put the verb into the right form.

1. (décorer) Nous ____________________ la salle de classe pour la fête.
2. (colorier) Les élèves ____________________ la carte de France.
3. (jouer) Martine ____________________ avec ses poupées.
4. (chanter) Est-ce que tu ____________________ à la chorale?
5. (regarder) Je ____________________ toujours les dessins animés.
6. (étudier) Les garçons ____________________ le français après les classes.
7. (parler) Est-ce que vous ____________________ au téléphone?
8. (copier) Paul ____________________ les questions.
9. (donner) Nous ____________________ un cadeau au professeur.
10. (danser) Les filles ____________________ dans le gymnase.
11. (arriver) J'____________________ à l'école en auto.
12. (aimer) Vous ____________________ le chocolat?
13. (détester) Nous ____________________ les légumes.
14. (dessiner) Je ____________________ le portrait de Maman.
15. (fermer) Tu ____________________ ta porte.
16. (montrer) Le professeur ____________________ les images dans le livre.
17. (marcher) Ils ____________________ dans le couloir.
18. (coller) Elle ____________________ le dessin dans son cahier.
19. (écouter) Paul et Anne ____________________ le disque.
20. (sauter) Nous ____________________ dans la cour.

NAME: ______________________________

EXERCISE E

Here are more sentences with verbs that you haven't met, but which you should find really easy! What do they mean?

1. (attaquer) L'armée ____________________ l'ennemi.
2. (demander) Nous ____________________ du chocolat.
3. (commander) Elles ____________________ du spaghetti au restaurant.
4. (entrer) Madame Lebrun ____________________ dans la salle de classe.
5. (développer) Le photographe ____________________ nos photos des vacances.
6. (sculpter) Monsieur Rodin ____________________ une belle statue.
7. (apprécier) Les spectateurs ____________________ le spectacle des Rolling Rocks.
8. (adorer) Nous ____________________ manger la pizza de Signor Esplosione.
9. (voyager) Est-ce que vous ____________________ en France cet été?
10. (tourner) Il ____________________ la clé pour ouvrir la porte.
11. (continuer) Nous ____________________ à jouer au football dans la salle de classe.
12. (ressembler) Monique ____________________ beaucoup à sa mère.
13. (collectionner) Mon frère ____________________ les cartes de baseball.
14. (habiter) Mes grands-parents ____________________ Vancouver.
15. (arranger) Maman ____________________ les fleurs dans le vase.
16. (quitter) Les spectateurs ____________________ le stade après le match.
17. (pousser) Vous ____________________ la porte pour entrer.
18. (séparer) Les élèves ____________________ les feuilles de papier.
19. (examiner) Le médecin ____________________ la jambe de Marcel.
20. (préparer) Maman ____________________ le déjeuner pour la famille.

Mamie and Papi's
Basic French Grammar

EXERCISE F

Now it's YOUR TURN!
Using any 20 *-er* verbs that you have learned, create 20 fabulously interesting sentences! Here are some extra verbs you might like to try!

dîner	visiter	occuper	accepter	proposer
analyser	déguiser	opposer	inviter	sauver

- 2 -

REGULAR -IR VERBS (PRESENT)

Question! Why do we call them *-ir* verbs?

Good question!

Answer: They end in *-ir* in their basic or *infinitive* form.

The *infinitive* of the verb is the "to _______" form,
e.g. to finish, to choose, to grow.

In English, we don't use the infinitive after a subject. If you said "I to choose" to your friends, they would laugh at you, right?

Here's the easy part! They don't do that in French either!

So what rules do these "action words" follow?

First let us ask you a question! What is wrong with the following?

he choose   she grow

Of course you know the answer; the verbs need an ENDING. In this case, the ending is 's'.

he choose**s**   she grow**s**

Guess what? You do the same in French, but with more endings!

So do you just add the endings to the *infinitive*?

NOOOOOOO!

First you take off the *-ir* part. That leaves you with what we call the **stem** of the verb. (the ending is the flower?)

So: if the infinitive of the verb is ***finir***, the stem is ***fin-.***

Then add the endings (each subject adds its own ending).

Singular	Plural
je fin**is**	nous fin**issons**
tu fin**is**	vous fin**issez**
il fin**it**	ils fin**issent**
elle fin**it**	elles fin**issent**

Here are 15 of them for you to learn and to use immediately!

		noircir	to blacken
abolir	to abolish	**jaunir**	to turn yellow
blanchir	to whiten	**pâlir**	to turn pale
choisir	to choose	**polir**	to polish
démolir	to demolish	**refroidir**	to chill
grandir	to grow	**rougir**	to blush, to turn red
grossir	to grow fat, to put on weight	**saisir**	to seize
maigrir	to grow thin, to slim	**verdir**	to grow green, to turn green

Note how many of them are formed from adjectives (especially of colour).

USEFUL NOTE!

An interesting and helpful fact is that lots of English verbs that end with the syllable "-ish" are *-ir* verbs in French. Here are a few French verbs; what is the English for them? (Don't forget the "to__________".)

établir ______________ fournir ______________

brandir ______________ chérir ______________

Here are four English verbs. Write down the French equivalent!

to finish ______________ to abolish ______________

to punish ______________ to polish ______________

EXERCISE G

Complete these verbs in the present tense:

finir (il)	____________	établir (vous)	____________
choisir (tu)	____________	rougir (il)	____________
démolir (elle)	____________	jaunir (elle)	____________
polir (je)	____________	grandir (tu)	____________
punir (nous)	____________	maigrir (je)	____________
abolir (ils)	____________	grossir (ils)	____________
finir (elle)	____________	polir (il)	____________
choisir (ils)	____________		

CRAZY -IR VERBS!

(We really mean irregular verbs that don't follow the same pattern as the others!)

There are 6 useful verbs that you must learn!

dormir (to sleep)	**mentir** (to tell lies)	**partir** (to leave, to go away)
sentir (to feel)	**servir** (to serve)	**sortir** (to go out)

How do you form them? Well, for the first three persons *(je, tu, il / elle)*, you not only remove the *-ir*, but also the last consonant before you add the ending. Watch this!

je dor**s**	tu dor**s**	il dor**t**	elle dor**t**
je par**s**	tu par**s**	il par**t**	elle par**t**

But the consonant goes back in for the last three persons *(nous, vous, ils / elles)* Note also that the endings are all different from the regular *-ir* verbs.

nous dorm**ons**	vous dorm**ez**	ils dorm**ent**	elles dorm**ent**
nous part**ons**	vous part**ez**	ils part**ent**	elles part**ent**

Get the idea? Now why don't you do the other verbs?

mentir		**sortir**		**servir**		**sentir**	
je	________	je	________	je	________	je	________
tu	________	tu	________	tu	________	tu	________
il	________	il	________	il	________	il	________
elle	________	elle	________	elle	________	elle	________
nous	________	nous	________	nous	________	nous	________
vous	________	vous	________	vous	________	vous	________
ils	________	ils	________	ils	________	ils	________
elles	________	elles	________	elles	________	elles	________

There! You're writing your own grammar book!

Exercise time!

EXERCISE H

A. Complete these regular *-ir* verbs as indicated:

(sortir) tu ____	(finir) elles ____	(choisir) je ____
(rougir) il ____	(partir) vous ____	(servir) il ____
(démolir) nous ____	(abolir) ils ____	(punir) je ____
(sentir) tu ____	(polir) elle ____	(grandir) ils ____
(grossir) je ____	(mentir) tu ____	(sortir) vous ____
(partir) il ____	(choisir) nous ____	(jaunir) il ____
(maigrir) nous ____	(servir) je ____	(blanchir) elle ____

B.Complete these irregular (crazy!) *-ir* verbs as indicated:

(sortir) il ____	(servir) ils ____	(mentir) elles ____
(partir) tu ____	(dormir) vous ____	(servir) nous ____
(sentir) nous ____	(dormir) elle ____	(sentir) vous ____
(mentir) je ____	(partir) je ____	(sortir) ils ____

EXERCISE 1

Put the correct form of the verb in the space provided.
Do you know what the sentence means? If not, find out!

1. (bâtir) Ils ________________ une nouvelle bibliothèque en ville.
2. (réfléchir) Elle ________________ sur les résultats de son examen.
3. (obéir) Tous les enfants ________________ à leurs parents, n'est-ce pas?
4. (réunir) La fête ________________ tous les anciens élèves de notre école.
5. (accomplir) Tu ________________ beaucoup si tu travailles bien.
6. (atterrir) L'avion ________________ à six heures et demie.
7. (grandir) Les petits enfants ________________ vite!
8. (élargir) Les ouvriers ________________ la rue devant notre maison.
9. (jaunir) Tu ________________! Tu es malade?
10. (chérir) Mamie et Papi ________________ leurs petites filles.

EXERCISE J

Here are some sentences with a choice of verbs. Choose the verb that best suits the meaning (not the silly one!) and then put the right ending on it to form a proper sentence:

1. (finir / punir) La classe ____________________ à onze heures et demie.
2. (partir / servir) Le train ____________________ à dix heures et quart.
3. (maigrir / grossir) Tu ____________________ si tu manges trop de frites!
4. (abolir / jaunir) En automne les feuilles ____________________ et tombent des arbres.
5. (sentir / démolir) Les ouvriers ____________________ la vieille école.
6. (sortir / dormir) Nous ____________________ du magasin avec nos achats.
7. (polir / mentir) Ce n'est pas vrai! Tu ____________________!
8. (rougir / établir) Elle est embarrassée; elle ____________________.
9. (punir / servir) Maman ____________________ le dîner à six heures.
10. (choisir / pâlir) Voici le fantôme. Tu ____________________?
11. (mentir / bâtir) Le garçon ____________________ une maison avec son Lego.
12. (jaunir / atterrir) L'avion du président ____________________ en ce moment.
13. (accomplir / finir) Il ____________________ beaucoup dans son travail.
14. (chérir / démolir) Nous ____________________ notre famille et nos amis.
15. (bleuir / obéir) Le soldat ____________________ toujours à ses ordres.
16. (abolir / sentir) Le tyran ____________________ les droits de ses sujets.
17. (grossir / blanchir) Maman ____________________ les draps.
18. (maigrir / réussir) Il ____________________ bien à l'examen avec une bonne note.
19. (vomir / sortir) Le volcan ____________________ la fumée dans l'air.
20. (partir / obéir) Le train ____________________ de la gare centrale.

EXERCISE K

Now for some creativity! Make 20 interesting sentences using the *-ir* verbs (regular and irregular) that you have learned.

____

____

____

____

____

____

____

____

____

____

____

____

____

____

____

____

____

____

____

____

- 3 -

REGULAR -RE VERBS (PRESENT)

Question! Why do we call them *-re* verbs?

Good question!

Answer: They end in *-re* in their basic or *infinitive* form.

The *infinitive* of the verb is the “to _______” form.
e.g. to sell, to answer, to hear

In English, we don’t use the infinitive after a subject. If you said “I to hear” to your friends, they would laugh at you, right?

Here’s the easy part! They don’t do that in French either!

So what rules do these “action words” follow?

First let us ask you a question! What is wrong with the following?

he sell   she lose

Of course you know the answer; the verbs need an ending. In this case, the ending is ‘s’.

he sell**s**   she lose**s**

Guess what? You do the same in French, but with more endings!

So do you just add the endings to the *infinitive*?

NOOOOOOO!

First you take off the -re part. That leaves you with what we call the **stem** of the verb. (the ending is the flower?)

So:
1) take the infinitive of this verb: *vend**re*** and remove ***-re.***

2) the stem is *vend-.*

3) then add the endings (each subject adds its own ending).

Singular	Plural
je vend**s**	nous vend**ons**
tu vend**s**	vous vend**ez**
il vend (No ending?)	ils vend**ent**
elle vend (That's correct!)	elles vend**ent**

PRONUNCIATION NOTE:
The endings of the singular forms are NOT PRONOUNCED.
The '*nous*' and '*vous*' form endings are pronounced, of course.
The 'd' of "*ils/elles vendent*" is pronounced, but the ending isn't.

Here are 10 *-re* verbs for you to learn and to use immediately!

attendre	to wait for	**pendre**	to hang
dépendre	to depend	**perdre**	to lose
descendre	to go down, to descend	**rendre**	to give back
entendre	to hear	**répondre**	to answer, to reply
mordre	to bite	**vendre**	to sell

OK, time for some exercises! Yayyyyyyyyyyyyy!

EXERCISE L

Put the correct ending on the verb. Write the complete form of the verb.

(attendre) il ________________

(descendre) nous ________________

(rendre) il ________________

(répondre) tu ________________

(vendre) je ________________

(perdre) nous ________________

(mordre) elle ________________

(entendre) vous ________________

(pendre) elles ________________

(dépendre) tu ________________

(entendre) ils ________________

(vendre) vous ________________

(descendre) je ________________

(répondre) elle ________________

(perdre) il ________________

EXERCISE M

Papi, you're WRONG! Papi got them all wrong. Can you correct these verbs for him?

1. Nous attendez ______________________________
2. Ils perdons ______________________________
3. Elle pends ______________________________
4. Tu perd ______________________________
5. Ils attendons ______________________________
6. Elle perdez ______________________________
7. Nous descend ______________________________
8. Ils dépends ______________________________
9. Je vend ______________________________
10. Vous pendons ______________________________

EXERCISE N

Now, let's make some sentences using these verbs:

1. (attendre) Elle ________________ ses amis devant le cinéma.
2. (vendre) Est-ce que tu ________________ ta voiture?
3. (entendre) Nous ________________ le bruit d'une explosion derrière l'école.
4. (pendre) Ils ________________ leurs vêtements dans le placard.
5. (perdre) Je ne joue pas bien au tennis; je ________________ toujours.
6. (rendre) Nous ________________ les livres à la bibliothèque.
7. (mordre) Mon chien est gentil; il ne ________________ pas.
8. (répondre) Le père de Jean ________________ au téléphone quand j'appelle.
9. (descendre) Nous ________________ dans les cavernes pour voir les stalactites.
10. (attendre) Est-ce que vous ________________ les résultats de l'examen?
11. (vendre) La mère de Simon ________________ sa bicyclette.
12. (répondre) Les élèves ________________ aux questions du prof.
13. (pendre) Mon frère ________________ le tableau au mur du salon.
14. (perdre) Je ________________ toujours mes mitaines en hiver.
15. (descendre) Ils ________________ de la tour Eiffel après leur visite au sommet.

Mamie and Papi's
Basic French Grammar

EXERCISE O

Can you supply the correct form of the missing *-re* verbs to make a sensible sentence?

1. Ils ________________ de belles robes chez Dior.
2. Vous ________________ quel train?
3. Nous ________________ un bruit étrange dans le sous-sol!
4. Marie ________________ contrôle de sa bicyclette.
5. Vous ________________ oui ou non?
6. Mon ami ________________ dans la caverne profonde.
7. Je ________________ ce livre à la bibliothèque.
8. Elles ________________ leurs vêtements dans l'armoire.
9. Nous ________________ la triste nouvelle du désastre.
10. Les filles ________________ bien à toutes les questions.
11. L'avion ________________ lentement vers l'aéroport.
12. Papi ________________ toujours quand il joue au tennis!
13. J'________________ mes amis devant le cinéma.
14. Mes soeurs ________________ impatiemment les résultats de leur examen.
15. Il ________________ dans son sandwich; il a faim!

Mamie and Papi's
Basic French Grammar

EXERCISE P

Now it's your turn! Make at least 10 interesting sentences using the *-re* verbs you have learned.

Mamie and Papi's
Basic French Grammar

- 4 -

IRREGULAR -ER VERBS

-ER VERBS WITH ATTITUDE!

So far, you have learned that all *-er* verbs follow the same pattern of endings, and behave themselves properly.

On the other hand, some groups of *-er* verbs do not quite follow the rules.
They change their stem in front of certain endings.

1. GROUP A - EASY ONES!

Verbs whose infinitives end in *-ger* have to ensure that the 'g' sounds are always soft. This is done already by the 'e' that follows the 'g' in most cases. However, there is one ending that does not begin with 'e'. Which one is it?

You got it! It's the *-ons* ending of the '*nous*' form! Bravo! Give yourself a prize!

So how do we give it a soft sound like the others?

We simply add an '*e*' in front of the *-ons*.

Here are a few examples:

manger (to eat):	je mange, nous mangeons
nager (to swim):	tu nages, nous nageons
voyager (to travel):	il voyage, nous voyageons
encourager (to encourage):	vous encouragez, nous encourageons
arranger (to arrange):	ils arrangent, nous arrangeons

Do you see how there must always be an 'e' after the '*g*'?

A similar group of verbs have an infinitive ending in *-cer*. However, instead of adding an '*e*' after the '*c*', the '*nous*' form adds a cedilla (looks like a 5 without the top line, or a worm on a hook!) to the '*c*'. It looks like this;

ç

So:

commencer (to start):	je commence, nous commen**ç**ons
lancer (to throw):	tu lances, nous lan**ç**ons
effacer (to erase):	il efface, nous effa**ç**ons
agacer (to annoy):	vous agacez, nous aga**ç**ons
lacer (to lace):	ils lacent, nous la**ç**ons
annoncer (to announce):	elles annoncent, nous annon**ç**ons

Let's do a quick exercise so that you'll have no problems with them.

EXERCISE Q

Add the correct endings to these verbs, making sure you watch for the '*nous*' forms that require special treatment:

(lancer) il ______________________

(lacer) elles ______________________

(nager) elle ______________________

(encourager) il ______________________

(voyager) tu ______________________

(agacer) nous ______________________

(annoncer) nous ______________________

(manger) nous ______________________

(effacer) vous ______________________

(tracer) nous ______________________

(prononcer) il ______________________

(arranger) nous ______________________

NAME: ______________________

GROUP B: VERBS THAT ADD AN ACCENT

With this group, as with the next groups, there is one question you ask first:
Is the ending pronounced?

Which endings are pronounced? *-ons* and *-ez* of course! You're so right!

Verbs like **lever**, **mener**, **acheter**, **geler**, **peler**, add a grave accent: *è* if the ending is NOT pronounced.

Here are some examples:

je lève **tu mènes** **il gèle** **elles achètent**

BUT

nous levons **vous menez** **nous achetons** **vous gelez**

OK, here's an exercise. Remember; what question do you ask first? What do you do if the answer is NO?

EXERCISE R

Write the correct form of the verb:

(acheter) ils ______________	(lever) elle ______________
(lever) nous ______________	(geler) il ______________
(acheter) nous ______________	(amener) tu ______________
(acheter) elles ______________	(lever) vous ______________
(geler) nous ______________	(lever) il ______________

All 10 right? Well done!

GROUP C: VERBS THAT CHANGE AN ACCENT

?

What question do you ask?

Is the ending pronounced?

If it isn't, then with these verbs, the accent changes from an *é* to an *è*

répéter (to repeat, to rehearse): **je répète, tu répètes**, *but* **nous répétons, vous répétez**

espérer (to hope): **j'espère, il espère**, *but* **nous espérons, vous espérez**

préférer (to prefer): **ils préfèrent, je préfère**, *but* **nous préférons, vous préférez**

OK, here's an exercise. Remember; what question do you ask first? What do you do if the answer is "no"? Make sure the accent is going the proper way! Not straight up and down!

EXERCISE S

(répéter) ils ____________________ (espérer) nous ____________________

(espérer) il ____________________ (préférer) vous ____________________

(répéter) tu ____________________ (répéter) nous ____________________

(espérer) elles ____________________ (préférer) je ____________________

(préférer) tu ____________________ (espérer) ils ____________________

GROUP D: VERBS THAT DOUBLE A CONSONANT

? What question do you ask?

Is the ending pronounced?

If it isn't, then with these verbs the last consonant is doubled..

jeter (to throw): **je jette, tu jettes,** *but* **nous jetons, vous jetez**

appeler (to call): **il appelle, elles appellent,** *but* **nous appelons, vous appelez**

OK, here's an exercise. Remember; what question do you ask first? What do you do if the answer is "no"?

EXERCISE T

(appeler) il ____________________

(jeter) elles ____________________

(appeler) tu ____________________

(jeter) vous ____________________

(appeler) nous ____________________

(jeter) il ____________________

GROUP E: -YER VERBS

?

What question do you ask?

Is the ending pronounced?

Si on ne prononce pas la terminaison, on change le *'y'* en *'i'*.

If the ending is not pronounced, the *'y'* changes to an *'i'*.

payer (to pay): **je paie, tu paies,** *but* **nous payons, vous payez**

essayer (to try): **il essaie, ils essaient,** *but* **nous essayons, vous essayez**

envoyer (to send): **elle envoie, elles envoient,** *but* **nous envoyons, vous envoyez**

OK, here's an exercise. Remember; what question do you ask first? What do you do if the answer is NO?

EXERCISE U

(payer) nous ____________________

(essayer) vous ____________________

(essayer) ils ____________________

(essayer) elle ____________________

(envoyer) ils ____________________

(envoyer) vous ____________________

(payer) il ____________________

(envoyer) tu ____________________

(payer) je ____________________

(essayer) nous ____________________

There! Easy, isn't it?

Mamie and Papi's
Basic French Grammar

GROUP F

Now here's a really crazy (but useful) set of verbs!
Here are their infinitives:

ouvrir (to open),

couvrir (to cover),

découvrir (to discover, to uncover),

offrir (to offer),

souffrir (to suffer)

These verbs have an identity problem. Their infinitive makes them look like *-ir* verbs, but in fact they take their endings from the *-er* verbs. Talk about crazy!

j'ouvr**e**

tu ouvr**es**

il ouvr**e**

elle ouvr**e**

nous ouvr**ons**

vous ouvr**ez**

ils ouvr**ent**

elles ouvr**ent**

EXERCISE V

(découvrir) je ____________________ (souffrir) elle ____________________

(ouvrir) nous ____________________ (couvrir) tu ____________________

(offrir) elles ____________________ (découvrir) ils ____________________

(souffrir) vous ____________________ (ouvrir) elle ____________________

(offrir) nous ____________________ (couvrir) il ____________________

NAME: ______________________________

Now, here's everything in one go! Can you figure them out?

What question do you ask first? Write it out on the following line!

____

What do you do if the answer is "no"?

EXERCISE W

(espérer) ils ______________________

(jeter) ils ______________________

(acheter) nous ______________________

(changer) nous ______________________

(payer) ils ______________________

(appeler) nous ______________________

(ouvrir) elle ______________________

(nager) nous ______________________

(mener) il ______________________

(promener) ils ______________________

(préférer) elle ______________________

(acheter) elles ______________________

(annoncer) nous ______________________

(nager) elles ______________________

(essayer) vous ______________________

(appeler) il ______________________

(geler) tu ______________________

(répéter) je ______________________

(lever) vous ______________________

(prononcer) nous ______________________

EXERCISE X

Now let's put the verbs in sentences that mean something!

1. (répéter) Elles ____________________ la chanson pour le concert.

2. (nager) Nous ____________________ dans le lac en été.

3. (lever) Elle ____________________ la main pour donner la réponse.

4. (ouvrir) Vous ____________________ la porte pour le professeur.

5. (préférer) Je ____________________ les films d'horreur.

6. (souffrir) Est-ce que tu ____________________ d'une fièvre?

7. (acheter) Elle ____________________ une robe bleue pour son anniversaire.

8. (promener) Ils ____________________ le chien dans le parc.

9. (encourager) Vous ____________________ l'équipe de basket-ball.

10. (payer) Elle ____________________ les billets pour le cinéma.

11. (appeler) Il ____________________ son ami au téléphone.

12. (jeter) Je ____________________ la balle au chien.

13. (préférer) Marie ____________________ aller au match.

14. (offrir) Martin et ses amis ____________________ un cadeau à sa mère.

15. (commencer) Les vacances ____________________ demain.

16. (lacer) Thomas et moi ____________________ nos patins pour aller sur la glace.

17. (acheter) Est-ce que tu ____________________ le cahier rouge?

18. (découvrir) Madame Lebrun ____________________ un tigre dans son placard.

19. (geler) Le poisson ____________________ dans le congélateur.

20. (essayer) Marguerite ____________________ sa nouvelle robe.

EXERCISE Y

Now it's your turn. Make at least 10 interesting sentences using the verbs you have learned recently.

- 5 -

ÉCRIRE, LIRE, DIRE, RIRE

Here are four verbs that follow a pattern in the singular forms, but are all different in their plural forms. You have to learn the differences. What a pain!

dire - to say, tell	**écrire** - to write	**lire** - to read	**rire** - to laugh
je dis	j'écris	je lis	je ris
tu dis	tu écris	tu lis	tu ris
il dit	il écrit	il lit	il rit
elle dit	elle écrit	elle lit	elle rit

Now for the different ones!

nous disons	nous écrivons	nous lisons	nous rions
vous dites	vous écrivez	vous lisez	vous riez
ils disent	ils écrivent	ils lisent	ils rient
elles disent	elles écrivent	elles lisent	elles rient

EXERCISE 2

We think that you can learn these verbs in 10 minutes flat!
Ready? Go for it!

Mamie and Papi's
Basic French Grammar

EXERCISE AA

Complete the following with the correct form of the verb without peeking at the right answer!

(lire) nous ________	(dire) elle ________	(écrire) tu ________
(dire) elles ________	(rire) ils ________	(lire) elle ________
(rire) vous ________	(dire) vous ________	(rire) nous ________
(écrire) nous ________	(dire) ils ________	(rire) tu ________
(lire) je ________	(écrire) elle ________	(dire) tu ________
(dire) elles ________	(lire) il ________	(écrire) vous ________
(rire) tu ________	(lire) vous ________	(dire) nous ________
(écrire) il ________	(lire) elles ________	(écrire) ils ________
(dire) je ________	(lire) nous ________	(écrire) je ________

EXERCISE BB

Papi, you're WRONG! Correct Papi's mistakes according to the subject.

1. je dit ____________
2. il lis ____________
3. ils écrisent ____________
4. tu ries ____________
5. tu dit ____________
6. vous disez ____________
7. elles écrisent ____________
8. nous risons ____________
9. il dis ____________
10. nous lisez ____________

ÉCRIRE, LIRE, DIRE, RIRE

EXERCISE CC

Write the correct form of the verb in the following sentences:

1. (dire) Marc est très honnête; il _______________ toujours la vérité.
2. (lire) Nous _______________ une excellente histoire dans la classe d'anglais.
3. (rire) Quand je vais au cirque, je _______________ quand je regarde les clowns.
4. (écrire) Marie _______________ une longue lettre à son amie Élodie.
5. (écrire) Nous _____________ des phrases intéressantes pour le prof de français!
6. (dire) Vous _______________ que vous aimez les maths?
7. (rire) Mes amis _______________ quand je raconte une blague amusante.
8. (lire) Je _______________ le journal tous les jours.
9. (écrire) Tu _______________ une lettre à tes parents?
10. (rire) Ils _______________ quand le comédien glisse sur la peau de banane.
11. (lire) Vous _______________ un roman passionnant?
12. (dire) Ils _______________ que le film est très bon.
13. (dire) Nous _______________ que nos amis sont très gentils.
14. (lire) Il _______________ dans le journal le reportage du dernier match.
15. (écrire) Elles _______________ les notes dans leur cahier.

EXERCISE DD

Complete each sentence with the correct verb.

1. Marie _______________ un beau roman d'Alexandre Dumas.
2. Quand les clowns se disputent, nous _______________.
3. Elles _______________ de jolies cartes de Noël pour leurs amis.
4. Qu'est-ce que tu _______________ dans le journal?
5. Le prof _______________ que les résultats de l'examen sont excellents.
6. Tu _______________ cette lettre au Premier Ministre?
7. Je _______________ que tu as tort, Papi!
8. Je pleure quand je _______________ une histoire d'amour tragique.
9. Nous _______________ une longue liste de demandes au père Noël!
10. Elles _______________ que le film est minable!

ÉCRIRE, LIRE, DIRE, RIRE

EXERCISE EE

Now for something creative! Write 20 fascinating sentences using the four verbs you have learned.

REVIEW 1

Write the correct form of the verb on the present tense.

1. (aimer) Vous ____________________ le chocolat?
2. (réfléchir) Elle ________________________ sur les résultats de son examen.
3. (attendre) Est-ce que vous ___________________ les résultats de l'examen?
4. (jaunir) Tu _______________________! Tu es malade?
5. (décorer) Nous ___________________ la salle de classe pour la fête.
6. (grandir) Les petits enfants ________________________ vite!
7. (étudier) Les garçons ____________________ le français après les classes.
8. (vendre) La mère de Simon ___________________ sa bicyclette.
9. (arriver) J'____________________ à l'école en auto.
10. (collectionner) Mon frère ____________________ les cartes de baseball.
11. (perdre) Je ___________________ toujours mes mitaines en hiver.
12. (voyager) Est-ce que vous ____________________ en France cet été?
13. (chanter) Est-ce que tu ____________________ à la chorale?
14. (entendre) Nous ___________________ le bruit d'une explosion derrière l'école.
15. (pendre) Ils ___________________ leurs vêtements dans le placard.

REVIEW 2

Write the correct form of the verb on the present tense.

1. (répéter) Elle ____________________ la chanson pour le concert.
2. (nager) Nous ____________________ dans le lac en été.
3. (lire) Tu ___________ un roman passionnant?
4. (lever) Elle ____________________ la main pour donner la réponse.
5. (dire) Vous ___________ que vous aimez les maths?
6. (ouvrir) Il ____________________ la porte pour le professeur.
7. (préférer) Ils ____________________ les films d'horreur.
8. (rire) Mes amis ___________ quand je raconte une blague amusante.
9. (écrire) Nous ___________ les notes dans leur cahier.
10. (acheter) Elle ____________________ une robe bleue pour la fête.
11. (promener) Elle ____________________ le chien dans le parc.
12. (encourager) Nous ____________________ l'équipe de basket-ball.
13. (payer) Elle ____________________ les billets pour le concert.
14. (jeter) Je ____________________ la balle au chien.
15. (préférer) Marie ____________________ aller au match.
16. (offrir) Martin et ses amis ____________________ un cadeau à sa mère.
17. (commencer) Les vacances ____________________ demain.
18. (lacer) Thomas et moi ____________________ nos patins pour aller sur la glace.
19. (geler) Le poisson ____________________ dans le congélateur.
20. (essayer) Marguerite ____________________ sa nouvelle jupe.

Mamie and Papi's Basic French Grammar

REVIEW 3

Write the correct form of the verb on the present tense.

1. (aimer) Tu ____________________ le chocolat?
2. (réfléchir) Il ________________________ sur les résultats de son examen.
3. (attendre) Est-ce que vous ____________________ les résultats de l'examen?
4. (écrire) Tu ___________ une lettre à tes parents?
5. (jaunir) Tu ________________________! Tu es malade?
6. (lire) Je ___________ le journal tous les jours.
7. (décorer) Vous ____________________ la salle de classe pour la fête.
8. (grandir) Les petits enfants ________________________ vite!
9. (étudier) Nous ____________________ le français après les classes.
10. (vendre) Je ____________________ ma bicyclette.
11. (arriver) Nous ____________________ à l'école en auto.
12. (dire) Vous ___________ que vous aimez les maths?
13. (collectionner) Mon ami ____________________ les cartes de baseball.
14. (perdre) Il ____________________ toujours mes mitaines en hiver.
15. (voyager) Est-ce que vous ____________________ en France cet été?
16. (appeler) Il ____________________ son ami au téléphone.
17. (entendre) Nous ____________________ le bruit d'une explosion derrière l'école.
18. (pendre) Elles ____________________ leurs vêtements dans le placard.
19. (préférer) Marie ____________________ aller au match.
20. (commencer) Nous ____________________ maintenant.

ANSWER KEY

Exercise A page 8

je chante
tu écoutes
elles adorent
nous sautons
ils arrivent
nous donnons
vous marchez
je décore
ils montrent
elle ferme
il déteste
tu fermes
nous fermons
ils découpent
je parle
elle colorie
nous regardons
il colle
elle saute
elles aiment

Exercise B page 9

calculez	jouent
étudie	déteste
chantez	donne
dessinons	marches
écoutent	colle
montrent	ferme
découpons	arrivons
parles	étudiez
jouent	dansons
sautent	regardez

Exercise C page 10

Il aime	nous chantons
elles jouent	il étudie
tu sautes	nous dansons
nous fermons	je découpe
elles marchent	ils donnent
tu arrives	ils collent
nous dessinons	j'aime
nous copions	vous détestez
il découpe	elle parle
tu écoutes	je montre

Exercise D page 11

1. décorons
2. colorient
3. joue
4. chantes
5. regarde
6. étudient
7. parlez
8. copie
9. donnons
10. dansent
11. arrive
12. aimez
13. détestons
14. dessine
15. fermes
16. montre
17. marchent
18. colle
19. écoutent
20. sautons

Exercise E page 12

1. attaque
2. demandons
3. commandent
4. entre
5. développe
6. sculpte
7. apprécient
8. adorons
9. voyagez
10. tourne
11. continuons
12. ressemble
13. collectionne
14. habitent
15. arrange
16. quittent
17. poussez
18. séparent
19. examine
20. prépare

Mamie and Papi's
Basic French Grammar

ANSWER KEY

Exercise G page 17

finit	établissez
choisis	rougit
démolit	jaunit
polis	grandis
punissons	maigris
abolissent	grossissent
finit	polit
choisissent	

page 18

mentir	**sortir**	**servir**	**sentir**
mens	sors	sers	sens
mens	sors	sers	sens
ment	sort	sert	sent
ment	sort	sert	sent
mentons	sortons	servons	sentons
mentez	sortez	servez	sentez
mentent	sortent	servent	sentent
mentent	sortent	servent	sentent

Exercise Ha page 19

sors	finissent	choisis
rougit	partez	sert
démolissons	abolissent	punis
sens	polit	grandissent
grossis	mens	sortez
part	choisissons	jaunit
maigrissons	sers	blanchit

Exercise Hb page 19

sort	servent	mentent
pars	dormez	servons
sentons	dort	sentez
mens	pars	sortent

Exercise I page 20

1. bâtissent
2. réfléchit
3. obéissent
4. réunit
5. accomplis
6. atterrit
7. grandissent
8. élargissent
9. jaunis
10. chérissent

Exercise J page 21

1. finit
2. part
3. grossis
4. jaunissent
5. démolissent
6. sortons
7. mens
8. rougit
9. sert
10. pâlis
11. bâtit
12. atterrit
13. accomplit
14. chérissons
15. obéit
16. abolit
17. blanchit
18. réussit
19. vomit
20. part

ANSWER KEY

Exercise L page 25

attend	pendent
descendons	dépends
rend	entendent
réponds	vendez
vends	descends
perdons	répond
mord	perd
entendez	

Exercise M page 25

1. attendons
2. perdent
3. pend
4. perds
5. attendent
6. perd
7. descendons
8. dépendent
9. vends
10. pendez

Exercise N page 26

1. attend
2. vends
3. entendons
4. pendent
5. perds
6. rendons
7. mord
8. répond
9. descendons
10. attendez
11. vend
12. répondent
13. pend
14. perds
15. descendent

Exercise O page 27

1. vendent
2. attendez
3. entendons
4. perd
5. répondez
6. descend
7. rends
8. pendent
9. entendons
10. répondent
11. descend
12. perd
13. attends
14. attendent
15. mord

Exercise Q page 30

lance	annonçons
lacent	mangeons
nage	effacez
encourage	traçons
voyages	prononce
agaçons	arrangeons

Exercise R page 31

achètent	lève
levons	gèle
achetons	amènes
achètent	levez
gelons	lève

ANSWER KEY

Exercise S page 32

répètent	espérons
espère	préférez
répètes	répétons
espèrent	préfère
préfères	espèrent

Exercise T page 33

appelle	jetez
jettent	appelons
appelles	jette

Exercise U page 34

payons	envoyez
essayez	paie
essaient	envoies
essaie	paie
envoient	essayons

Exercise V page 35

découvre	souffre
ouvrons	couvres
offrent	découvrent
souffrez	ouvre
offrons	couvre

Exercise W page 36

espèrent	préfère
jettent	achètent
achetons	annonçons
changeons	nagent
paient	essayez
appelons	appelle
ouvre	gèles
nageons	répète
mène	levez
promènent	prononçons

Exercise X page 37

1. répètent
2. nageons
3. lève
4. ouvrez
5. préfère
6. souffres
7. achète
8. promènent
9. encouragez
10. paie
11. appelle
12. jette
13. préfère
14. offrent
15. commencent
16. laçons
17. achètes
18. découvre
19. gèle
20. essaie

Exercise AA page 40

lisons	dit	écris
disent	rient	lit
riez	dites	rions
écrivons	disent	ris
lis	écrit	dis
disent	lit	écrivez
ris	lisez	disons
écrit	lisent	écrivent
dis	lisons	écris

ANSWER KEY

Exercise BB page 40

1. dis
2. lit
3. écrivent
4. ris
5. dis
6. dites
7. écrivent
8. rions
9. dit
10. lisons

Exercise CC page 41

1. dit
2. lisons
3. ris
4. écrit
5. écrivons
6. dites
7. rient
8. lis
9. écris
10. rient
11. lisez
12. disent
13. disons
14. lit
15. écrivent

Exercise DD page 42

1. lit
2. rions
3. écrivent
4. lis
5. dit
6. lis
7. dis
8. lis
9. écrivons
10. disent

Review 1 page 44

1. aimez
2. réfléchit
3. attendez
4. jaunis
5. décorons
6. grandissent
7. étudient
8. vend
9. arrive
10. collectionne
11. perds
12. voyagez
13. chantes
14. entendons
15. pendent

Review 2 page 45

1. répète
2. nageons
3. lis
4. lève
5. dites
6. ouvre
7. préfèrent
8. rient
9. écrivons
10. achète
11. promène
12. encourageons
13. paie
14. jette
15. préfère
16. offrent
17. commencent
18. laçons
19. gèle
20. essayez

Review 3 page 46

1. aimes
2. réfléchit
3. attendez
4. écris
5. jaunis
6. lis
7. décorez
8. grandissent
9. étudions
10. vends
11. arrivons
12. dites
13. collectionne
14. perd
15. voyagez
16. appelle
17. entendons
18. pendent
19. préfère
20. commençons

Lightning Source UK Ltd.
Milton Keynes UK
UKOW06f0254230814

237404UK00002B/22/P